HEALING LIGHT

THIRTY MESSAGES OF
LOVE, HOPE, AND COURAGE

ALEXANDRA VILLARD DE BORCHGRAVE

PREFACE BY
K. NATWAR SINGH

FOREWORD BY
BOUTROS BOUTROS-GHALI

MJF Books
New York

Published by MJF Books
Fine Communications
322 Eighth Avenue
New York, NY 10001

Healing Light
LC Control Number: 2011932140
ISBN-13: 978-1-60671-082-1
ISBN-10: 1-60671-082-6

Printed in Singapore.

MJF Books and the MJF colophon are
trademarks of Fine Creative Media, Inc.

TWP   10   9   8   7   6   5   4   3   2   1

DEDICATION

For all those who have suffered
the adversity of life:

Let the light of the moon
bathe my soul in peace
And cause inner calm
my sorrow to cease.

Let the rays of the sun
bring radiance to my life
And lead my fresh spirit
to where hope is rife.

Alexandra Villard de Borchgrave

CONTENTS

PREFACE
K. Natwar Singh

FOREWORD
Boutros Boutros-Ghali

INTRODUCTION
Alexandra Villard de Borchgrave

AWAKENINGS

Garden of Light

Gift of Life

Gesture of Love

Morning Light

Swallow in Flight

Sunlit Place

Overcome All Sorrow

Balance of Life

ARISINGS

Finding Joy

Stream of Love

Gather All the Children

Beyond Myself

Forgiveness

Mountains in the Mist

Perseverance

Courage

Redemption

ARTWORKS

ACKNOWLEDGMENTS

PREFACE

On rare occasions one comes across a book
that captures spirituality, beauty, and a universal
message in a single volume. *Healing Light* by
Alexandra Villard de Borchgrave is such a book.

The author's vision of humanity, peace, and love
is put forth in her evocative words, which she has
married with distinctive and unusually appropriate
Indian Mughal art paintings, bringing East and
West together in an extraordinary display. This
wonderful pairing of poetry with beautiful imagery
epitomizes the spirit of India.

Healing Light is above all an inspirational reflection
of a cosmic connectivity that binds the human race
together in its quest for ultimate understanding:
One that transcends all creeds and cultures.

K. Natwar Singh
Minister for External Affairs
India

FOREWORD

I belong to the Arab world for whose people poetry has, for centuries, been one of the most important forms of expression of their emotions, of their hopes, of their sorrow.

I have found in Alexandra Villard de Borchgrave's moving poems this same universal dimension of poetry, which should be the language of dialogue, of conciliation, and of peace between all nations and civilizations.

To all those who are seeking inspiration in these troubled times of fear, despair, mistrust, and incomprehension, I recommend they read this remarkable collection of poems which represent an oasis of compassion and inner calm.

Boutros Boutros-Ghali
Secretary General of the United Nations
1992 — 1996

INTRODUCTION

The peace and clarity of the early morning light may be shattered in a second by a natural disaster, an act of terror, the loss of a loved one, or a devastating illness, creating suffering for which we truly need the courage of a lion.

The second anniversary of September 11, 2001, dawned as poignantly clear as that fine, crisp September 11 when the hijacked planes struck the World Trade Center towers and the Pentagon with deadly intent.

As I watched the ceremonies begin at Ground Zero, I felt increasing sadness as the children came forward one by one to call out their lost parents' names. The grief and longing etched on their small faces left an imprint on my heart that gave birth two days later to prayers for them in the form of poems that flowed out in rhyme at all hours of the day and night. Within a month I had written thirty prayers.

One day, my dear friend and Indian art scholar, Eleni Philon, whose husband, Alexander Philon, had served as the Greek ambassador to India and then Washington, came by for tea. I showed her my efforts and, with her characteristic warmth, she said, "You know, these prayers are not just for children, they are for all of us. They are so Sufi in concept that I think Indian Mughal art would be the perfect way to illustrate them. I would like to take them to India with me and send you some samples."

Those few kind words transformed my work. When I received the first copies of the exquisite sixteenth- and seventeenth-century paintings Eleni had chosen, I knew I had found the ideal visual counterpoints to my words. Just as my poems spoke of details within ourselves of courage, perseverance, love, and faith, so the details of the emotive animals, brilliant stars, and glorious flowers within the miniatures conveyed the same emotions and completed my message.

Soon I was spending hours researching Indian Mughal, Pahari, and Rajasthani art at the Freer and Sackler Galleries. Having never seen the paintings before writing the prayers, I was particularly moved, as I discovered image after image mirroring my words, by artists hundreds of years ago in India seeing the world in the same light as an American woman in Washington in the twenty-first century.

W. B. Yeats wrote in 1912 that in Indian tradition, "poetry and religion are the same thing" and that the symbols of petals, dust, or an empty house within the poetry are "images of the heart turning to God." These messages expressed through poetry are for all those who strive to overcome the adversity of life and who seek comfort, joy, strength, and hope to meet the challenges facing us today.

May the humanity within our souls lead us to overcome the misunderstandings between us and to creating peace and compassion for all mankind.

Alexandra Villard de Borchgrave

AWAKENINGS

Crystallize my existence

        in a drop of dew

Sparkling, ephemeral

        with strivings of every hue.

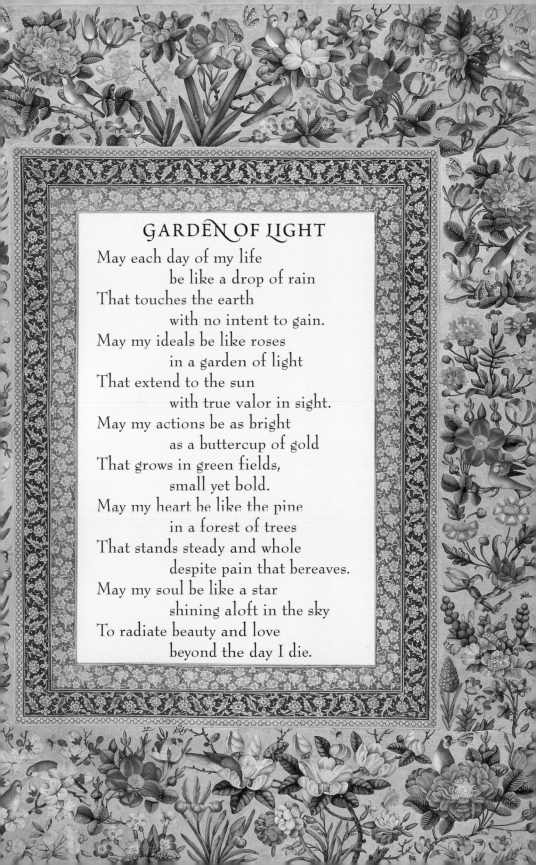

GARDEN OF LIGHT

May each day of my life
       be like a drop of rain
That touches the earth
       with no intent to gain.
May my ideals be like roses
       in a garden of light
That extend to the sun
       with true valor in sight.
May my actions be as bright
       as a buttercup of gold
That grows in green fields,
       small yet bold.
May my heart be like the pine
       in a forest of trees
That stands steady and whole
       despite pain that bereaves.
May my soul be like a star
       shining aloft in the sky
To radiate beauty and love
       beyond the day I die.

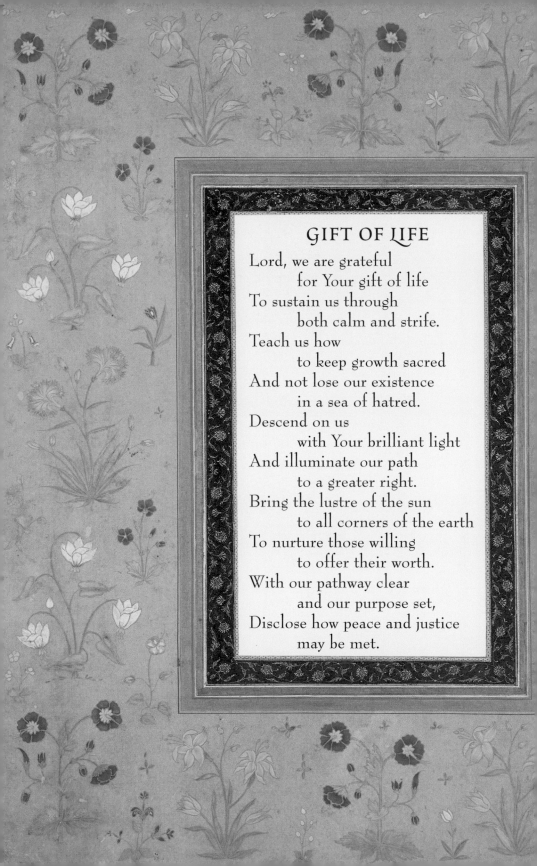

GIFT OF LIFE

Lord, we are grateful
   for Your gift of life
To sustain us through
   both calm and strife.
Teach us how
   to keep growth sacred
And not lose our existence
   in a sea of hatred.
Descend on us
   with Your brilliant light
And illuminate our path
   to a greater right.
Bring the lustre of the sun
   to all corners of the earth
To nurture those willing
   to offer their worth.
With our pathway clear
   and our purpose set,
Disclose how peace and justice
   may be met.

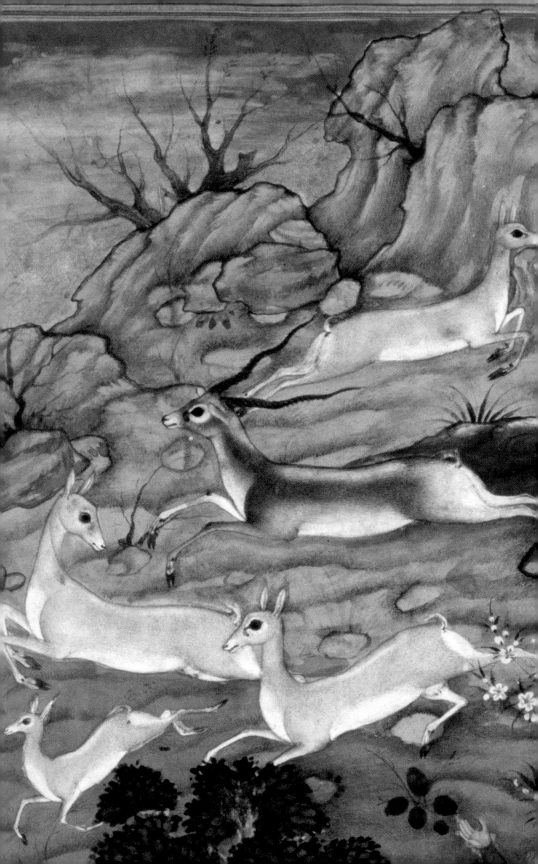

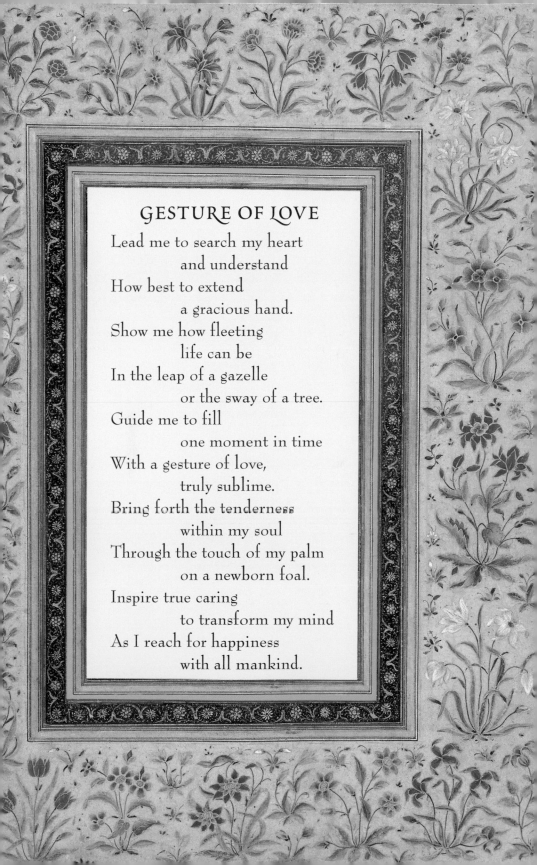

GESTURE OF LOVE

Lead me to search my heart
      and understand
How best to extend
      a gracious hand.
Show me how fleeting
      life can be
In the leap of a gazelle
      or the sway of a tree.
Guide me to fill
      one moment in time
With a gesture of love,
      truly sublime.
Bring forth the tenderness
      within my soul
Through the touch of my palm
      on a newborn foal.
Inspire true caring
      to transform my mind
As I reach for happiness
      with all mankind.

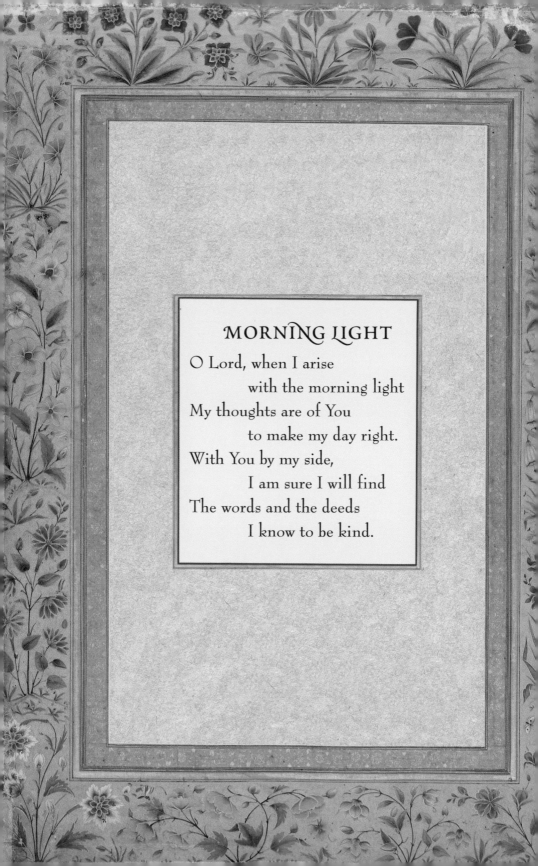

MORNING LIGHT

O Lord, when I arise
      with the morning light
My thoughts are of You
      to make my day right.
With You by my side,
      I am sure I will find
The words and the deeds
      I know to be kind.

SWALLOW IN FLIGHT

Let kindness grow within me
      when my day has begun
Like a flower opens its heart
      to the warmth of the sun.
Let grace guide my steps
      like a swallow in flight
As I seek a higher place
      upon which to alight.
Let hope be the wind
      that fills my sail
And keeps me as steady
      as the shell of a snail.
Let joy fill my spirit
      when I am touched by love
Whether it is as brief as the flutter
      of a white-winged dove.
Let compassion allow me
      to see those in need
Like the tree offers its shelter
      to the solitary seed.
Let wisdom be gained
      from each stone I've turned,
And bring peace with the night
      from lessons I've learned.

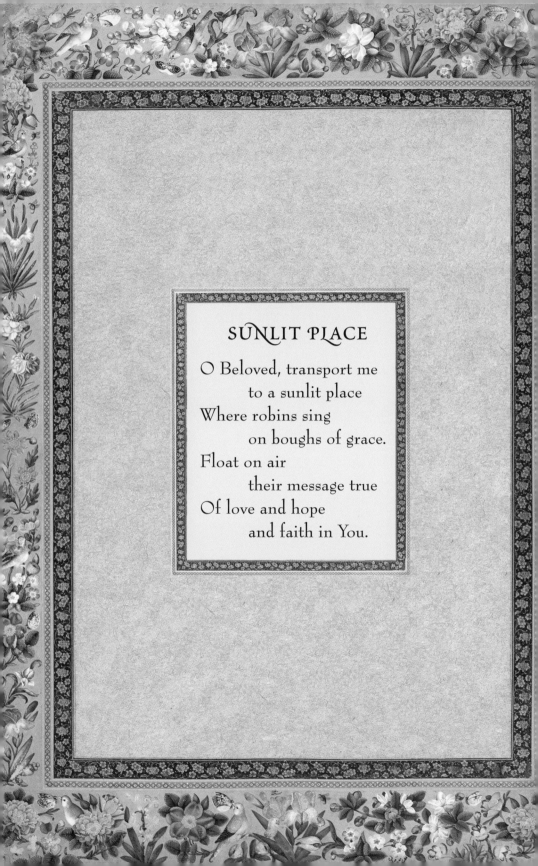

SUNLIT PLACE

O Beloved, transport me
　　to a sunlit place
Where robins sing
　　on boughs of grace.
Float on air
　　their message true
Of love and hope
　　and faith in You.

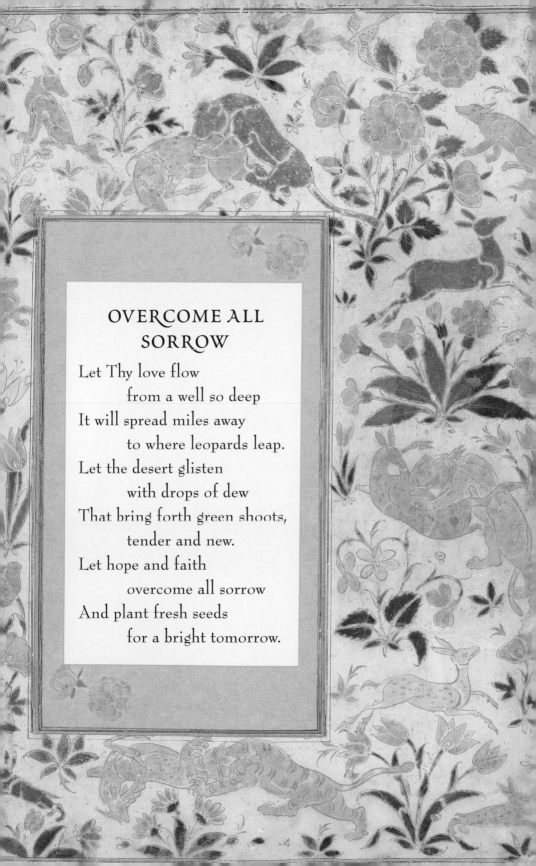

OVERCOME ALL
SORROW

Let Thy love flow
  from a well so deep
It will spread miles away
  to where leopards leap.
Let the desert glisten
  with drops of dew
That bring forth green shoots,
  tender and new.
Let hope and faith
  overcome all sorrow
And plant fresh seeds
  for a bright tomorrow.

BALANCE OF LIFE

Still my heart
      in its desire for flight
And make clear
      how best my emotions to fight.
Scatter my fears
      like petals in the heat
To warm the earth
      beneath my trembling feet.
Prove the resilience
      of the stem as it bends
With patience and resolve
      in a wind that rends.
Reveal the harmony
      between the rose and the bee
As I seek the balance of life
      on both land and sea.
Crystallize my existence
      in a drop of dew
Sparkling, ephemeral
      with strivings of every hue.
Ignite my soul
      with the kiss of the sun
And spur good deeds
      until my time has come.

ARISINGS

Let generosity well from the depths

of our hearts

Like a bubbling stream

that flows to all parts.

FINDING JOY

O Lord, help all those
    who have suffered this day
Find strength and joy
    along the way.
Let the warmth of Thy love
    dry the tears
And allow courage and hope
    to banish the fears.

STREAM OF LOVE

Let generosity well from the depths
       of our hearts
Like a bubbling stream
       that flows to all parts.
Let the cool, clear water
       restore and fulfill
All the hopes and dreams
       within us still.
Let the light of a star
       be captured at dawn
And nurtured with love
       like a delicate fawn.
Let a random act
       of true devotion
Be the one that sets
       healing events in motion.
Let each fleeting moment
       of love on earth
Bind us together
       with joy and mirth.

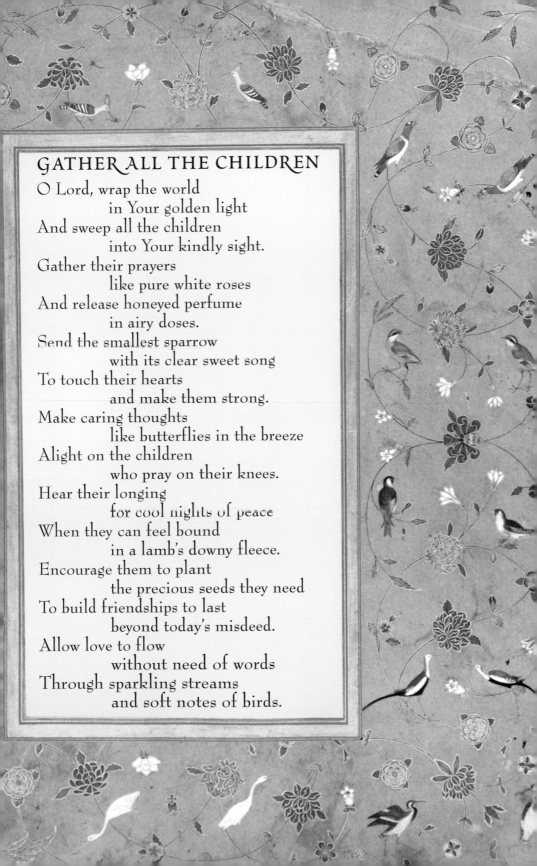

GATHER ALL THE CHILDREN

O Lord, wrap the world
       in Your golden light
And sweep all the children
       into Your kindly sight.
Gather their prayers
       like pure white roses
And release honeyed perfume
       in airy doses.
Send the smallest sparrow
       with its clear sweet song
To touch their hearts
       and make them strong.
Make caring thoughts
       like butterflies in the breeze
Alight on the children
       who pray on their knees.
Hear their longing
       for cool nights of peace
When they can feel bound
       in a lamb's downy fleece.
Encourage them to plant
       the precious seeds they need
To build friendships to last
       beyond today's misdeed.
Allow love to flow
       without need of words
Through sparkling streams
       and soft notes of birds.

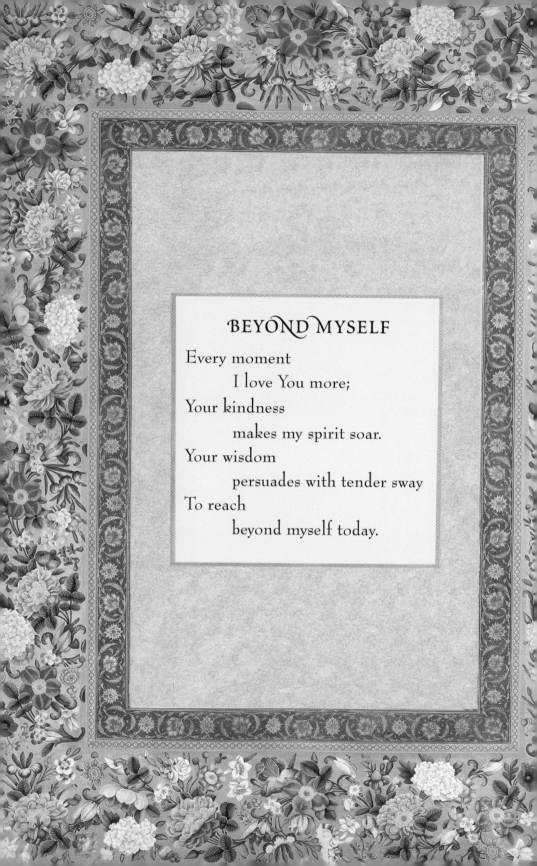

BEYOND MYSELF

Every moment
        I love You more;
Your kindness
        makes my spirit soar.
Your wisdom
        persuades with tender sway
To reach
        beyond myself today.

FORGIVENESS

I have been troubled
       on this day
And need Your forgiveness
       to keep my fears at bay.
My words were spoken
       in haste and outright
When reflection and restraint
       would have served my plight.
I honestly regret
       the distress I sowed
And ask Your pardon
       to embark on a new road.
I strive for perfection
       in whatever I do
And must accept my best
       when I am through.
Guide me to see
       it's the effort that counts
And ease my frustration
       when tension mounts.
I need to see the world
       as an imperfect place
Where all is not lost
       if I have lost a race.
Make me feel Your love
       in the depth of my heart
To begin a new day
       with a blithe, glad start.

MOUNTAINS IN THE MIST

Let me face tall mountains
          rising in the mist
With the courage and spirit
          to climb and insist.
Let me ply rough stones
          beneath my feet
As surely as a stallion,
          confident and fleet.
Let me seek the shade of the cypress
          along my path
To rally new efforts free
          of grief or wrath.
Let me see green grass
          in dark crevasses beyond
Like hope and clarity
          in a reflecting pond.
Let me find my quest
          to be for greater good
Bringing love to succeed
          where hate once stood.

PERSEVERANCE

May my eyes perceive the grace
       in petals on a stream
As I seek the gentle flow
       of a lucid waking dream.
May my lips taste the sweetness
       in the lingering honeyed dew
As I seek to smile through my sorrow
       and begin my task anew.
May my heart gather the strength
       from the roots of the willow tree
As I seek to persevere,
       rather than to flee.
May my feet step with the dignity
       of the blue-tipped stalking crane
As I seek a balanced path
       through the shadows of my pain.
May my being learn the humbleness
       of a single blade of grass
As I seek to walk with honor
       through the twists of life's morass.

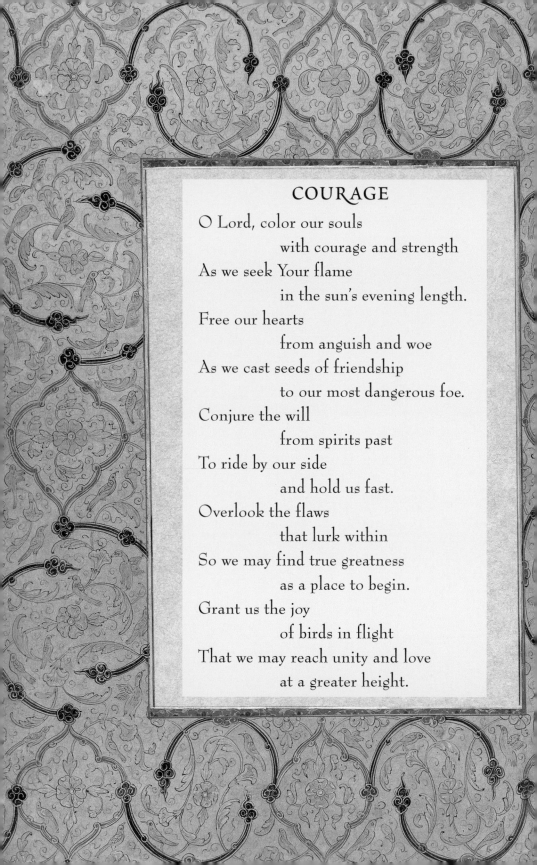

COURAGE

O Lord, color our souls
      with courage and strength
As we seek Your flame
      in the sun's evening length.
Free our hearts
      from anguish and woe
As we cast seeds of friendship
      to our most dangerous foe.
Conjure the will
      from spirits past
To ride by our side
      and hold us fast.
Overlook the flaws
      that lurk within
So we may find true greatness
      as a place to begin.
Grant us the joy
      of birds in flight
That we may reach unity and love
      at a greater height.

REDEMPTION

As I smolder like a fire
        in the center of the earth,
Let me find cool waters
        where I may prove my worth.
With honor and valor
        my companions in stride,
Let my actions and words
        dictate my pride.
Let truth and honesty
        lift me above
Those who would harm me
        and rob me of love.
Let the wind take my soul
        far into the sky
To a world way beyond
        my earthly cry.
Let me reach the ones
        who seek mercy here
To create a new spirit,
        free of anger or fear.
Let Your infinite power
        break through misconception
And shed light on the way
        to future redemption.

ABSOLUTIONS

Open my soul

        to Your radiant power

That I may rise with grace

        in this hour.

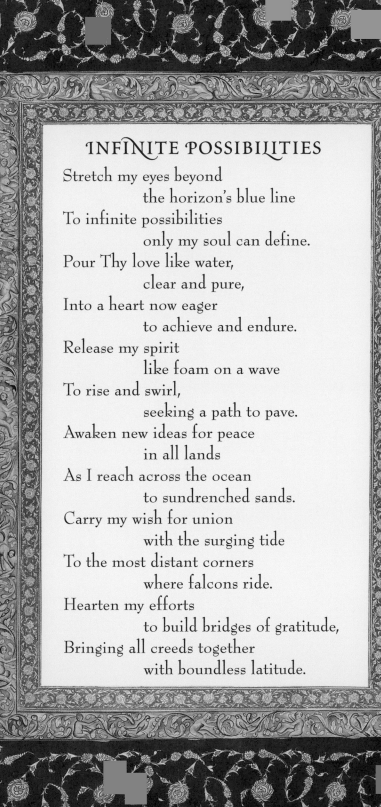

INFINITE POSSIBILITIES

Stretch my eyes beyond
      the horizon's blue line
To infinite possibilities
      only my soul can define.
Pour Thy love like water,
      clear and pure,
Into a heart now eager
      to achieve and endure.
Release my spirit
      like foam on a wave
To rise and swirl,
      seeking a path to pave.
Awaken new ideas for peace
      in all lands
As I reach across the ocean
      to sundrenched sands.
Carry my wish for union
      with the surging tide
To the most distant corners
      where falcons ride.
Hearten my efforts
      to build bridges of gratitude,
Bringing all creeds together
      with boundless latitude.

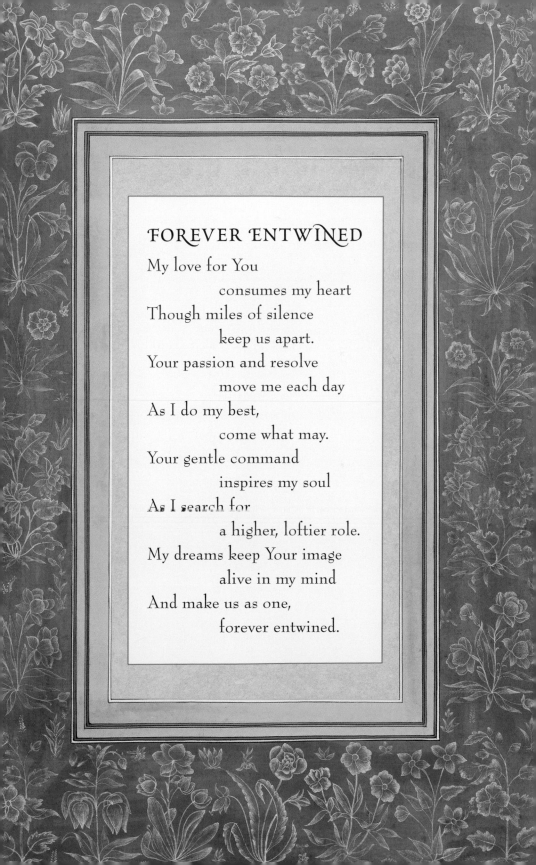

FOREVER ENTWINED

My love for You
        consumes my heart
Though miles of silence
        keep us apart.
Your passion and resolve
        move me each day
As I do my best,
        come what may.
Your gentle command
        inspires my soul
As I search for
        a higher, loftier role.
My dreams keep Your image
        alive in my mind
And make us as one,
        forever entwined.

SUDDEN GALE

When change descends
   like a sudden gale,
Let my spirit be first
   to stand and prevail.
When wind and rain
   challenge the sun,
Let my step remain firm
   until calm is won.
When hail and lightening
   threaten my role,
Let hope and possibility
   be my goal.
When the storm abates
   bringing sweet, clean air,
Let my mind discern clearly
   what is true and fair.
When the lone evening star
   emerges at last,
Let serenity rule
   the future I cast.

RISE WITH GRACE

O Lord, set the stars to be
> my companions tonight

And fill my empty heart
> with their lustrous light.

Cast their shimmering dust
> upon my face

To halt the tears
> that run apace.

My longing is great
> for a love beyond measure

As I strive to discover
> life's inner treasure.

The fire within me
> has fallen low

And I need the warmth
> only You can bestow.

Guide my spirit
> to an inner source

Where courage and faith
> may reset my course.

Open my soul
> to Your radiant power

So that I may rise with grace
> in this hour.

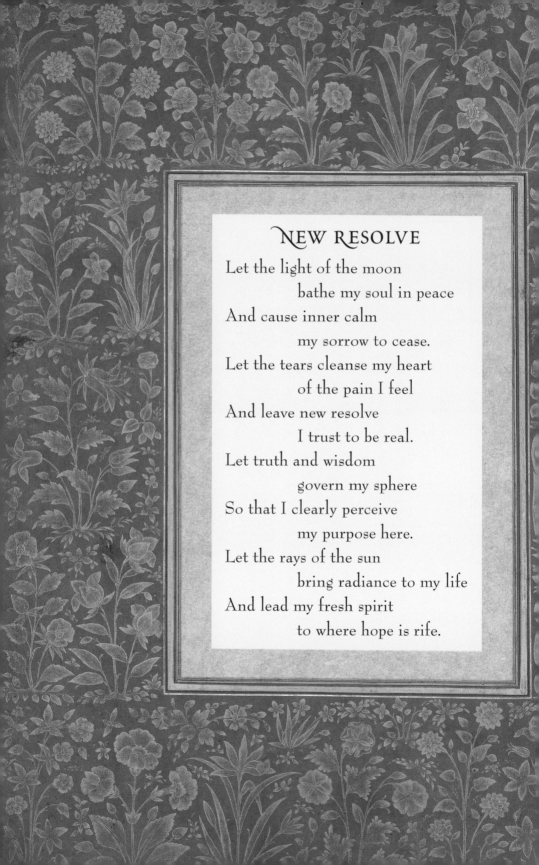

NEW RESOLVE

Let the light of the moon
       bathe my soul in peace
And cause inner calm
       my sorrow to cease.
Let the tears cleanse my heart
       of the pain I feel
And leave new resolve
       I trust to be real.
Let truth and wisdom
       govern my sphere
So that I clearly perceive
       my purpose here.
Let the rays of the sun
       bring radiance to my life
And lead my fresh spirit
       to where hope is rife.

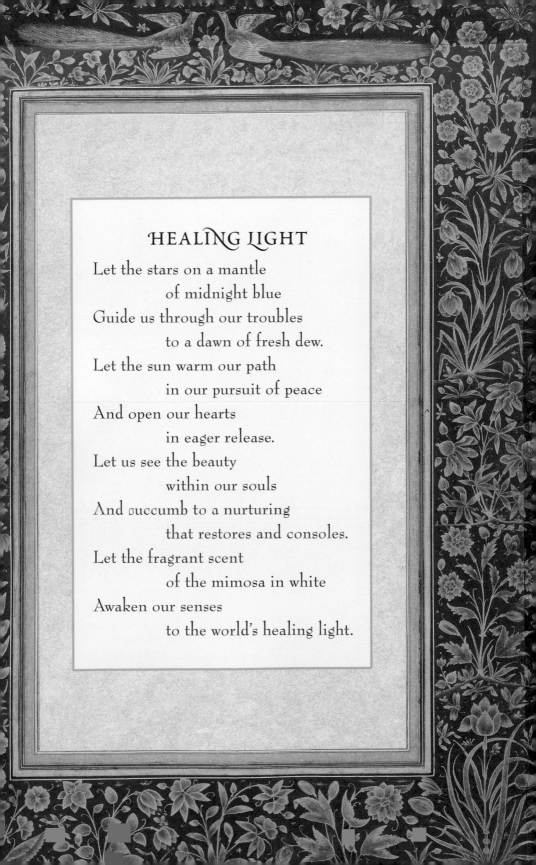

HEALING LIGHT

Let the stars on a mantle
        of midnight blue
Guide us through our troubles
        to a dawn of fresh dew.
Let the sun warm our path
        in our pursuit of peace
And open our hearts
        in eager release.
Let us see the beauty
        within our souls
And succumb to a nurturing
        that restores and consoles.
Let the fragrant scent
        of the mimosa in white
Awaken our senses
        to the world's healing light.

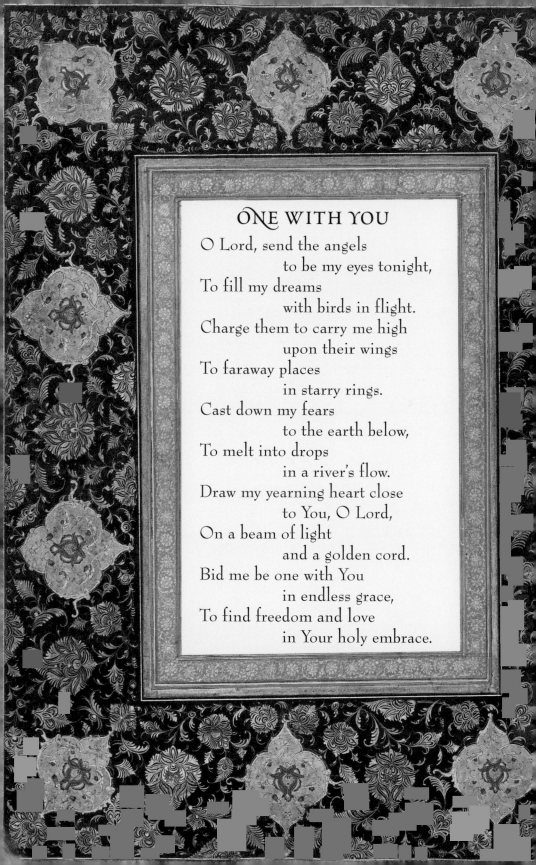

ONE WITH YOU

O Lord, send the angels
        to be my eyes tonight,
To fill my dreams
        with birds in flight.
Charge them to carry me high
        upon their wings
To faraway places
        in starry rings.
Cast down my fears
        to the earth below,
To melt into drops
        in a river's flow.
Draw my yearning heart close
        to You, O Lord,
On a beam of light
        and a golden cord.
Bid me be one with You
        in endless grace,
To find freedom and love
        in Your holy embrace.

TRANQUILITY

Bind the fragments of my heart
    with hope and peace
As the butterfly soothes the petal
    of a flower soon to cease.
Draw forth the strength
    beneath woe's dark shade
As moonlight breaks through the trees
    of a verdant, secret glade.
Urge me not to yearn
    for that which I cannot have
And instead trust in Your wisdom
    to provide a gentle salve.
Show me Your love
    in a young deer's sable eyes
As I enter the grassy lair
    where tranquility lies.

ARTWORKS

GARDEN OF LIGHT

Border detail

Top: Jahangir entertains Shah Abbas. Page from the St. Petersburg Album. (South Asian, Mughal, ca. 1620. Courtesy of the Freer Gallery of Art, Smithsonian Institution, Washington, D.C.: Purchase, F1942.16a)

Right: Allegorical representation of Emperor Jahangir and Shah Abbas of Persia. Page from the St. Petersburg Album. Abu'l Hasan. (South Asian, Mughal, ca. 1618. Courtesy of the Freer Gallery of Art, Smithsonian Institution, Washington, D.C.: Purchase, F1945.9a)

GARDEN OF LIGHT

GIFT OF LIFE

GESTURE OF LOVE

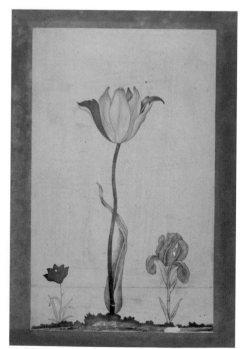

GIFT OF LIFE

Top Left: Page from the dispersed album compiled for Shah Jahan. (India, Mughal, ca. 1650. Hashem Khosrovani Private Collection)

Top right: Akbar hunts with trained cheetahs from the Akbarnama. La'l and Sanwala. (India, ca. 1590-95. Courtesy of V&A Images, Victoria and Albert Museum, London, England)

Left: Two Tulips and an Iris. (India, Shah Jahan period, ca. 1645. Private Collection. © The Trustees of the British Museum)

GESTURE OF LOVE

MORNÍNG LIGHT

Top left: A bird. Muhammad. (South Asian, Mughal, 17TH century. Courtesy of the Freer Gallery of Art, Smithsonian Institution, Washington, D.C.: Purchase, F1939.47b)

Top right: Calligraphy. (South Asian, Mughal, ca. 1650. Courtesy of the Freer Gallery of Art, Smithsonian Institution, Washington, D.C.: Purchase, F1948.28b)

Right:
Jahangir entertains Shah Abbas. Page from the St. Petersburg Album. (South Asian, Mughal, ca. 1620. Courtesy of the Freer Gallery of Art, Smithsonian Institution, Washington, D.C.: Purchase, F1942.16a)

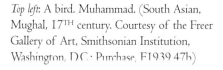

Border detail

MORNÍNG LIGHT

SWALLOW IN FLIGHT

SUNLIT PLACE

SWALLOW IN FLIGHT

Top left: Madonna and Child
with Angels. From an album
of Emperor Jahangir. (India,
Mughal, ca. 1526-1858.
Courtesy of Harvard
University Art Museums,
Cambridge, Massachusetts.
[1958.233])

Top right: Shah Jahan honors
the religious orthodoxy.
Page from the St. Petersburg
Album. (South Asian, Mughal,
ca. 1635. Courtesy of the
Freer Gallery of Art,
Smithsonian Institution, Washington, D.C.:
Purchase, F1942.18a)

Left: Narada visits Valmiki. Episodes from the
Ramayana. (India, ca. 1775-1800. Courtesy of
The John and Berthe Ford Collection)

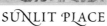

SUNLIT PLACE

OVERCOME ALL SORROW

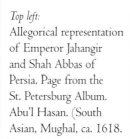

Border detail

Top left:
Allegorical representation of Emperor Jahangir and Shah Abbas of Persia. Page from the St. Petersburg Album. Abu'l Hasan. (South Asian, Mughal, ca. 1618. Courtesy of the Freer Gallery of Art, Smithsonian Institution, Washington, D.C.: Purchase, F1945.9a)

Top right: A lion hunt. (South Asian, Mughal, ca. 1600. Courtesy of the Freer Gallery of Art, Smithsonian Institution, Washington, D.C.: Purchase, F1946.17)

Right: The submission of Bairam Khan. Dharm Das. (South Asian, Mughal, ca. 1604. Courtesy of the Freer Gallery of Art, Smithsonian Institution, Washington, D.C.: Purchase, F1952.33)

OVERCOME ALL SORROW

FINDING JOY

FINDING JOY

Top left: The Elephant King attacked by the crocodile. (India, ca. 1650. Courtesy of The John and Berthe Ford Collection)

Top right and opposite page: A poem by Amir Shahi. Page from the late Shah Jahan Album. Mir-Ali Sultani. (South Asian, Mughal, 16TH century. Courtesy of the Arthur M. Sackler Gallery, Smithsonian Institution, Washington, D.C.: Purchase - Smithsonian Unrestricted Funds, Smithsonian Collections Acquisition Program and Dr. Arthur M. Sackler, S1986.90)

Details from this painting are also used on contents and divider pages.

Left: Shah Shuja. Page from the late Shah Jahan Album. (South Asian, Mughal, ca. 1650. Art & History Collection. Photography courtesy of the Arthur M. Sackler Gallery, Smithsonian Institution, Washington, D.C.: LTS1995.2.98)

BALANCE OF LIFE

STREAM OF LOVE

Top right: Shah Tahmasp in the Mountains. Farrukh Beg. (South Asian, Mughal, ca. 1620. Courtesy of the Freer Gallery of Art, Smithsonian Institution, Washington, D.C.: Purchase, F1939.47a)

Right: Bahram Gur watching Dilaram charm the wild animals with her music. Leaf from a Khamsa by Amir Khosrow Dihlavi (1253-1325). Artist: Miskin. (Indian. Paintings. Mughal, period of Akbar [1556-1605], 1597-98. Courtesy of The Metropolitan Museum of Art, Gift of Alexander Smith Cochran, 1913. [13.228.28] Photograph © 2001 The Metropolitan Museum of Art)

STREAM OF LOVE

GATHER ALL THE CHILDREN

BEYOND MYSELF

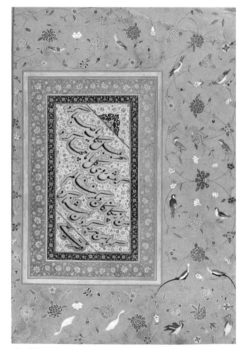

GATHER ALL THE CHILDREN

Top left: A Floral Fantasy. (Mughal or Deccani, ca. 1650. Private Collection. © The Trustees of the British Museum)

Top right: Jahangir entertains Shah Abbas. Page from the St. Petersburg Album. (South Asian, Mughal, ca. 1620. Courtesy of the Freer Gallery of Art, Smithsonian Institution, Washington, D.C.: Purchase, F1942.16a)

Left The Nightingale and the Rose. Calligraphy in Nastaliq. Signed by Faquir Ali, 16TH century. Border, Shah, Jahan Period, ca. 1640. (Hashem Khosrovani Private Collection)

BEYOND MYSELF

FORGIVENESS

Border detail

Top left: Allegorical representation of Emperor Jahangir and Shah Abbas of Persia. Page from the St. Petersburg Album. Abu'l Hasan. (South Asian, Mughal, ca. 1618. Courtesy of the Freer Gallery of Art, Smithsonian Institution, Washington, D.C.: Purchase, F1945.9a)

Top right: A Jeweled Woman Before a Palace Gateway. (Jaipur, late 18TH century. Courtesy of Christie's Images)

Right: Calligraphy. Mir Ali. (Calligraphy: Iran, ca. 1530-1550. Borders: South Asian, 17TH century. Courtesy of the Freer Gallery of Art, Smithsonian Institution, Washington, D.C.: Purchase, F1939.50b)

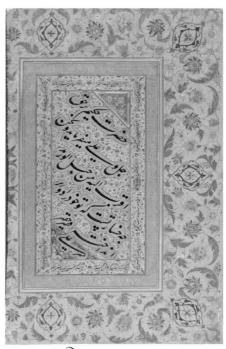

FORGIVENESS

MOUNTAINS IN THE MIST

MOUNTAINS IN THE MIST

PERSEVERANCE

Top left: The Dragon and the Simurgh. Attributed to Miskina. (Mughal, ca. 1595-1600. Courtesy of The British Museum, 1920-9.17.05)

Top right: Calligraphy. Page from the St. Petersburg Album. (South Asian, Mughal, ca. 1620. Courtesy of the Freer Gallery of Art, Smithsonian Institution, Washington, D.C.: Purchase, F1945.9b)

Left: Shri Krishna with the Flute. (South Asian, Pahari, ca. 1790-1800. Courtesy of the Freer Gallery of Art, Smithsonian Institution, Washington, D.C.: Purchase, F1930.83)

PERSEVERANCE

COURAGE

Top left: Four Portraits from the St. Petersburg Album. (South Asian, Mughal, ca. 1650-1660. Courtesy of the Arthur M. Sackler Gallery, Smithsonian Institution, Washington, D.C.: Purchase—Smithsonian Unrestricted Trust Funds, Smithsonian Collections Acquisition Program and Dr. Arthur M. Sackler. S1986.421b)

COURAGE

Top right: Equestrian Portrait of Shah Jahan. (South Asian, Rajput, ca. 1750-1770. Courtesy of the Arthur M. Sackler Gallery, Smithsonian Institution, Washington, D.C.: Purchase—Smithsonian Unrestricted Trust Funds, Smithsonian Collections Acquisition Program and Dr. Arthur M. Sackler, S1986.415)

Right: Maharana Sangram Singh Hunting Crane at Nahar Magra. (Udaipur, Rajasthan, India ca. 1720. Courtesy of National Gallery of Victoria, Melbourne, Australia. Felton Bequest, 1980)

REDEMPTION

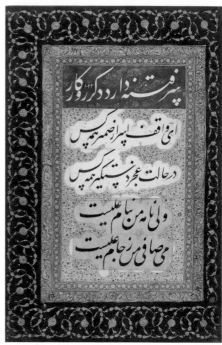

INFINITE POSSIBILITIES

REDEMPTION

Top left: Commissioned work from India. (India, 2004. Alexandra Villard de Borchgrave Private Collection)

Top right: Calligraphy. Mir Imad al-Husayni. Page from the St. Petersburg Album. Borders: Muhammad-Baqir and Muhammad-Hadi. (South Asian, Mughal, ca. 1660. Courtesy of the Freer Gallery of Art, Smithsonian Institution, Washington, D.C.: Purchase, F1996.1b)

Left: Image Caption: Arrows of Love Pierce His Weary Mind. Gitagovinda illustration. (India, ca. 1775-1780. Private Collection, Germany)

FOREVER ENTWINED

FOREVER ENTWINED

Top left: Commissioned work from India. (India, 2004. Alexandra Villard de Borchgrave Private Collection)

Top right: Toilette of Radha. (India, Pahari, Kangra School, ca. 1810-20. ©The Cleveland Museum of Art, Edward L. Whittemore Fund 1953.245)

Right: Krishna and Radha in Procession to a Palace Sunset. (Rajasthan, Nathadwara, ca. 1900. ©The Trustees of the British Museum)

INFINITE POSSIBILITIES

SUDDEN GALE

RISE WITH GRACE

SUDDEN GALE

Top left: Krishna and the Gopis Take Shelter from the Rain. Rajasthan, Jaipur, ca. 1760. Courtesy of The Metropolitan Museum of Art Purchase, Mr. and Mrs. John E. Wiley and Cynthia Hazen Polsky Gifts, and Rogers Fund, 1991 [1991.94]. Photograph © The Metropolitan Museum of Art, 1991)

Top right: Rama, Lakshmana, Vishmavitra. From a Persian translation of the Ramayana. Ghulam 'Ali. (South Asian, Mughal, late 16TH century. Courtesy of the Freer Gallery of Art, Smithsonian Institution, Washington, D.C.: Gift of Charles Lang Freer, F1907.271.34)

Left: Calligraphy. Page from the St. Petersburg Album. (South Asian, Mughal, ca. 1660-1670. Courtesy of the Freer Gallery of Art, Smithsonian Institution, Washington, D.C.: Purchase—Anonymous donor and the Friends of Asian Arts, F1994.4b)

RISE WITH GRACE

NEW RESOLVE

Top left: Calligraphy. Page from the St. Petersburg Album. Imad al-Hasani. (South Asian, Mughal, ca. 1608. Courtesy of the Freer Gallery of Art, Smithsonian Institution, Washington, D.C.: Purchase, F1942.16b)

Top right: Portrait of Abd ar-Rahim, Khan Khanan. Hashim. (South Asian, Mughal, ca. 1626. Courtesy of the Freer Gallery of Art, Smithsonian Institution, Washington, D.C.: Purchase, F1939.50a)

NEW RESOLVE

Right: The Gopis Search for Krishna from a Bhagavata Purana. Guler-Kangra. (South Asian, Pahari, ca. 1780. Courtesy of the Freer Gallery of Art, Smithsonian Institution,

HEALING LIGHT

ONE WITH YOU

HEALING LIGHT

Top left: Jahangir Holding
a Globe. Abu'l-Hasan
(Nadir al-Zaman).
(South Asian, Mughal,
ca. 1650. Courtesy of
the Freer Gallery of Art,
Smithsonian Institution,
Washington, D.C.:
Purchase, F1948.28a)

Top right: Two Deer in a
Landscape. (Early 19TH
century. Courtesy of the
Freer Gallery of Art,
Smithsonian Institution,
Washington, D.C.:
Purchase, F1939.48a)

Left: A Deer Hunt. (India, Rajasthan, Kotah, ca. 1775.
Courtesy of The Walters Art Museum, Baltimore,
Maryland. Photograph ©The John and Berthe Ford
Collection: Gift of John and Berthe Ford, 2000)

ONE WITH YOU

TRANQUILITY

Top left: Sheltering from the Rain. (India, Uttar Pradesh, Garhwal ca. 1775-1800. The John and Berthe Ford Collection)

Top right: Calligraphy. Page from the St. Petersburg Album. (South Asian, Mughal, 17TH century. Courtesy of the Freer Gallery of Art, Smithsonian Institution, Washington, D.C.: Purchase, F1942.18b)

Right: Rama Hunting by Moonlight. Bhimsen. (India, Rajasthan, Kotah, ca. 1781.

TRANQUILITY

Courtesy of the Arthur M. Sackler Museum, Harvard University Art Museums, Gift of Stuart Cary Welch, Jr., in memory of Jacqueline Bouvier Kennedy Onassis, 1995.102)

HEALING LIGHT FOR CHILDREN

NO HARM

NO HARM

PRECIOUS BIRTH

Opposite page: Gajendra Seized. From a Gajendramoksha series. (Udaipur, ca. 1680-90. Courtesy of Andrew Topsfield, Ashmolean Museum)

Top left: Art of the Past. (India, 18TH century. Subhash Kapoor Private Collection)

Top right: Commissioned work from India. (India, 2004. Alexandra Villard de Borchgrave Private Collection)

Right: Squirrels in a Plane Tree. Signed by Abu'l-Hasan (Nadir al-Zaman) (ca. 1610. Courtesy of The British Library, Johnson Album, I, No. 30)

PRECIOUS BIRTH

REACHING HEARTS

GARDEN OF LOVE

Top: Monkeys and Bears Investigate the Rikshabila Cave. Folio from the "Shangri" Ramayana. (India, Jammu and Kashmir, Bahu, ca. 1700-1710. Courtesy of the Los Angeles County Museum of Art, from the Nasli and Alice Heeramaneck Collection, Museum Associates Purchase, M.74.5.11)

Left: Commissioned work from India. (India, 2004. Alexandra Villard de Borchgrave Private Collection)

GARDEN OF LOVE

GUIDING ANGELS

Top left: Todi Ragini. (India, Rajasthan, ca. 1730-1750. Courtesy of the Arthur M. Sackler Museum, Harvard University Art Museums, Private Collection, 488.1983)

Top right: Shah Jahan with Asaf Khan from the late Shah Jahan Album. Bichitr. (South Asian, ca. 1650. Courtesy of the Arthur M. Sackler Gallery, Smithsonian Institution, Washington, D.C.: Purchase–Smithsonian Unrestricted Trust Funds, Smithsonian Collections Acquisition Program, and Dr. Arthur M. Sackler, S1986.403)

Right: Emperor Aurangzeb in a shaft of light with later floral border. Page from the St. Petersburg Album. Hunhar. Borders Muhammad Baqir and Muhammad-Hadi. (South Asian, Mughal, ca. 1660. Courtesy of the Freer Gallery of Art, Smithsonian Institution, Washington, D.C.: Purchase, F1996.1)

GUIDING ANGELS

Album Folio. (South Asia, India, Rajasthan, Mughal Period,
932-1274/1526-1. Courtesy of the Arthur M. Sackler
Museum, Harvard University Art Museums, Gift of John
Goelet Photographic Services. © 2004 President and
Fellows of Harvard College)

ACKNOWLEDGMENTS

The creation of *Healing Light*, both in the writing and the choosing of the illustrations, has been touched from the beginning by the extraordinary kindness of family, friends, and strangers.

First and foremost, this book would not have been possible without the exceptional courtesy of museums and private collectors all over the world.

I would like to extend a special note of recognition to The Freer Gallery of Art and the Arthur M. Sackler Gallery in Washington, DC, for the invaluable assistance that was extended to me during this entire project through the kindness of director Dr. Julian Raby and the entire staff, most notably Rebecca L. Barker, Dr. Massumeh Farhad, David Hogge, Carol Huh, Julia Keller, Kathryn Phillips, Linda Raditz, Reiko Yoshimura, and Katie Ziglar. I am especially grateful to Dr. Debra Diamond for her gracious guidance; to Neil Greentree for his superb photography; and to art scholar Pallavi Mansingh for her inspired research.

In addition, I am very appreciative of the help I received from Mary McWilliams, Kimberly Masteller, Stephanie Beck,

Jennifer Hughes, and photographer Katya Kallsen at The Sackler Museum at Harvard University.

I am truly indebted to all the curators, rights and reproductions coordinators, and visual resources heads of the museums and institutions that participated in this project, specifically The British Museum; The British Library; Christie's Images; The Cleveland Museum of Art; The Los Angeles County Museum; The Metropolitan Museum of Art; The Musée Guimet; The National Gallery of Art; The National Gallery of Victoria; The Rietberg Museum; The Royal Asiatic Society; Sotheby's; and The Victoria and Albert Museum.

My path was greatly facilitated by The Asia Society in New York, under the distinguished leadership of the president, Dr. Vishakha N. Desai, and The Asia Society Washington Center, under the able directorship of Joseph C. Snyder, and I am most grateful to them.

I was enlightened and enriched by many on my journey, but I wish to thank, in particular, Dr. Eberhard Fischer, John and Berthe Ford, Ken and Kitty Galbraith, Subhash Kapoor, Hashem Khosrovani, Kenneth Robbins, Dr. Konrad Seitz, Andrew Topsfield, and Stuart Carey Welch for their generosity in searching for and lending me the paintings, transparencies, and slides from their private collections. I acknowledge with gratitude the private collectors who generously agreed to lend me their works but wish to remain anonymous.

For assisting me in bringing the images together, I offer a special thank you to Cris McCarthy and the entire team at the Chrome photographic lab in Washington for their outstanding work; to

Bronwyn Latif in New Delhi for finding the talented artists who produced the unique endpapers and borders that show the ongoing tradition of miniature painting in India; to Patti Malone for her first splendid pages; and to Annemarie Feld for her beautiful design of the book.

My deepest thanks go to my publisher, Marta Hallett; to the team at Glitterati Incorporated, including Ima Ebong and Minju Pak; and to my agent Georges Borchardt and Deanna Heindel for believing in the project and for making *Healing Light* a reality. Nemir A. Kirdar once again offered generosity and wise counsel, and I am truly grateful for his kind consideration.

The wonderful friends who sustained, nurtured, and encouraged me with love, introductions, inspirational books, insights, daily calls, and visits in their beautiful homes are the mainstay of my life. I don't want to leave a single treasured person out, and so I thank every one of you, dear friends, with all my heart.

My whole family supported me at every step, but I reserve my most loving thanks for my beloved husband, Arnaud, for devotedly taking, without complaining, thoughtful minutes each day to spur me on my way.

And, finally, I had prayed for a project through which I could make a contribution, and I am deeply thankful for being filled with the desire to write prayers as poems for those saddened by the pain of life and for being led to see the spiritual treasures of the world.